PADDLING MICHIGAN'S PINE: TALES FROM THE RIVER

DOC FLETCHER

Sunrise on the Pine

AuthorHouse™
1663 Liberty Drive
Bloomington, IN 47403
www.authorhouse.com
Phone: 1-800-839-8640

Published by AuthorHouse 1/2/2014

ISBN: 978-1-4918-4873-9 (sc)
ISBN: 978-1-4918-4875-3 (e)

Library of Congress Control Number: 2013923512

Photographs: Doc Fletcher
Map: Maggie Meeker
Illustrations: Keith Jones aka bigtimeartguy

authorHOUSE®

CONTENTS

Class 2 rapids, 1 & ½ miles downstream from Peterson

PINE RIVER ACKNOWLEDGEMENTS

To Maggie for your love, your constant support, and for always giving me a reason to smile.

To Jonesey for your friendship and for drawings that always tell the story.

To Shoeless Jim Horina for the stories and for outfitting our expedition.

To Jack Forsberg for welcoming me to your writings and into your and Midge's home, for leading me down a steep hill with youthful abandon to introduce me to the beautiful Pine East Branch.

To Janice Cool Peterson for sharing your immense knowledge of the Pine and Tustin.

To Doug Galloup for allowing me to use your historic photos and walking me through the history of what was Edgetts.

To Mark Slavsky for introducing me to the story of the most important day of fishing our country has ever known.

To Gideon Gerhardt for fighting on behalf of all of us, ensuring our right to paddle or fish a river through privately-owned land.

To Lovells Township Historical Society (near Grayling) members Roger Fechner and Carol Britton for sharing the story of our once great fish - Michigan's Grayling.

To Jerry, Lori, and Jeff Horan for introducing us to the beautiful "Wildlife Intentions" and sharing the story of the town of Riverbank.

To Colleen Sexton for allowing me to reproduce the historic Wellston photos and telling me stories of the town and Inn's origin.

To Maggie, Toni, Christine & Co. for feeding the Pine River Expedition Crew aka the Crack Research Team, ensuring we were fueled and ready to explore the Pine.

To the Crack Research Team for their camaraderie and observations, and for taking canoeing & kayaking to another level of fun.

Dedicated to two Kirks...

Kirk Weideman and Kirk Pederson

One facing a life-long challenge,
one a challenge over the last few years.

Both meeting the challenge with strength,
good cheer, and a can-do spirit.

Both setting an example for all of us.

Outfitter used by the Pine River Expedition Team aka the Crack Research Team

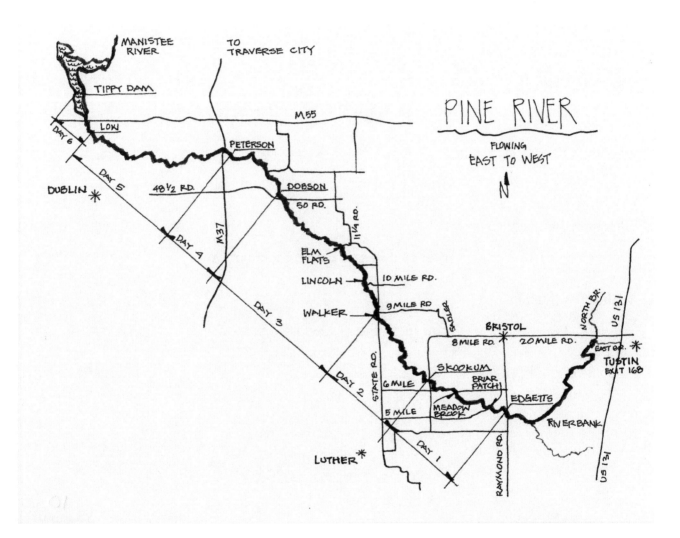

PINE RIVER: MILES AND MINUTES
BETWEEN PUBLIC ACCESS POINTS

From east to west...

1. Edgetts to Briar Patch   2 miles; 45 minutes

                    Total 2 miles; 45 minutes

2. Briar Patch to Meadowbrook   1.5 miles; 32 minutes

                    Total 3.5 miles; 1 hour 17 minutes

3. Meadowbrook to Skookum North   3.4 miles; 1 hour 3 minutes

                    Total 6.9 miles; 2 hours 20 minutes

4. Skookum North to Skookum South   .5 miles; 10 minutes

                    Total 7.4 miles; 2 hours 30 minutes

5. Skookum South to Walker   6.6 miles; 2 hours

                    Total 14 miles; 4 hours 30 minutes

6. Walker to Lincoln   2.5 miles; 37 minutes

                    Total 16.5 miles; 5 hours 7 minutes

7. Lincoln to Elm Flats   3 miles; 43 minutes

                    Total 19.5 miles; 5 hours 50 minutes

8. Elm Flats to Dobson   6.6 miles; 1 hour 40 minutes

                    Total 26.1 miles; 7 hours 30 minutes

9. Dobson to Peterson   6.3 miles; 1 hour 33 minutes

                    Total 32.4 miles; 9 hours 3 minutes

10. Peterson to Low   8.7 miles; 2 hours 12 minutes

                    Total 41.1 miles; 11 hours 15 minutes

11. Low to Norman-Dixon (Tippy Dam)   2.2 miles; 50 minutes

                    Total 43.3 miles; 12 hours 5 minutes

Dodging debris between Edgetts and Skookum

THE OTHER WONDERS

I want to go where the rivers flow
to the waterfalls of foam,
I want to go where the memories
are etched into my bones,
where the people I meet
are the friends I greet
good friends from long ago.

The city lights are exciting sights
to a man adventure bound,
but when you've stayed too long
the excitements gone,
it's time to be moving on.
so I'm hitting the trail and riding the rails
and pointing my feet toward home.

Now, I'm back from the rush of the world
of climbing the business hills,
of phones that never stop ringing
and the morning traffic that kills.

From days without enough hours
from deadlines that cannot be met
from bills that always need paying
and taxes that make a man sweat.

Do I miss the excitement of travel
and the applause of a job well done,
or the ego high of shared high fives
that come from a contract won?

If you're personal sail is an Alpha male
you're stuck with a quest to win,
so when it's time to go from fast to slow,
you're like a fish that's shed its fins.

Now I'm back to my place on the river,
where the Birch and Pine share the air,
where humming birds and newborn fawns
are but few of the wonders I share.

But life is always a trade-off
trading one for another,
I've had the one and all of its fun,
but now, I enjoy... the other.

by Jack Forsberg from his 2012 book "Beat The Anvil"

Jack Forsberg & his home along the Pine East Branch

Where the Pine begins: the merger of the East (L) and North (R) branches

THE PINE RIVER INTRODUCTION

The Pine is one of Michigan's most loved rivers. It runs clear, cold, clean, and is best known for its speed, its high quality trout fishing, & summer-time popularity w/ paddlers (for the best experience, go pre-Memorial Day & post-Labor Day & avoid summer weekends). The Pine has been designated: (1) a Michigan "Blue Ribbon Trout Stream", (2) a Michigan "Natural River" and (3) in its lower 26 miles, a U.S. Forest Service "National Wild & Scenic River".

This is not a beginner's river. The Pine's final 43 of its 60 miles are serviced by canoe & kayak liveries (rentals), and those 43 miles feature class 1 and 2 rapids throughout. Over the Pine's entire 60 miles, it has a gradient drop of 7' per mile, but over its final 43 miles the per mile drop in the river floor is among the Lower Peninsula's highest at almost 10' per mile with a maximum gradient drop of 20' in the 1st mile downstream from the Peterson access.

The high sandy banks of the lower Pine, along with the river's deep & rich riverside vegetation, provide a beautiful back drop to a canoe or kayak trip. Located in the northwest Lower Peninsula, the Pine is the best way to travel though the counties of Osceola, Lake, Wexford, and Manistee. The "Pine" name comes from the White Pine forests that were thick along its banks. In Michigan's logging days of the mid to late 1800s, the Pine River was known as the South Branch of the Manistee River. The Pine & Manistee Rivers meet in Manistee County, 5 minutes north of the small town of Wellston, a mile and a half above the east-west M55 highway. The confluence of the rivers takes place as both flow into the Tippy Dam Pond, east of Tippy Dam. On the west side of Tippy Dam, only one of these two great rivers continues its westward flow as the Pine is no more, its waters absorbed by the Manistee.

The headwaters of the Pine form 15 miles southwest of Cadillac and 3 miles west of Tustin, a community found 1 mile east of US131 exit 168. The river is created by the merger of two creeks, the East & the North Branches of the Pine, a few feet SW of 20 Mile Road & 220 Avenue. From this beginning, the Pine flows southwest and then it divots to the northwest until it ends at the Tippy Dam Pond north of Wellston. On its 60 mile journey, the Pine flows through or near the towns of Riverbank, the ghost town of Edgetts, and the small communities of Bristol, Luther, Hoxeyville, Dublin, and Wellston.

The first 17 miles of the Pine are not serviced by canoe & kayak liveries, and are full of logjams (keeping rivers free flowing are a service that the liveries provide to us all, whether we rent from them or not). Our attempt to paddle these 17 miles was very difficult and slow, taking 2 hours to cover the first mile. Obstructions we met at times forced portages across private property, introducing us to some upset homeowners. With respect to their feelings, we decided to abandon our plan to paddle the river's headwaters and instead journey only down that section of the river cleared and serviced by liveries.

This book then is about the final 43 of the Pine's 60 miles, i.e. the section of the river kept free-flowing by the 6 canoe & kayak liveries located along the river. Within these 43 miles are 12 public access points. In this book you will find listings of liveries, public access points, and campgrounds found along or near the Pine. For the 26 miles of the Lower Pine (beginning at Elm Flats), due to large summertime crowds, paddling permits are required by law from the Memorial Day Friday through Labor Day and are available at www.recreation.gov.

The final 43 miles of the river are broken up into 6 day trips, each day trip getting its own chapter, or travelogue. The daily travelogue notes miles and minutes from that day's start to finish, and from start to various landmarks along the way, letting you know how you are progressing against the daily total time/miles, as well as letting you know what to expect downstream. Also noted is each day's degree of paddling difficulty, a simple 3-step rating system: 1. Beginner, 2 Intermediate (the difference vs. beginner is "can you steer around/ through obstructions OR rapids?") and 3. Highly Skilled.

Note: the majority of our Pine paddling took place in the early spring, when the water runs deeper and faster. The time of year that you visit the river, as well as your paddling ability may effect how many minutes it takes to canoe or kayak each daily section, but the miles will stay the same. For each day trip, it is noted in what time of year the paddling took place, and if the river speed was "normal" or otherwise.

The Pine was full of Grayling until the 1890s, when they gradually died out after the big timber was cut. Once the Grayling were gone, the state stocked the river with brook, brown, and rainbow trout. Springs large and small, many superb trout streams on their own, feed the Pine and it stays cold enough for brook trout in the summer and warm enough for brown and rainbow in the winter. The cold, clean river agrees with the trout's natural reproduction and, since hatchery restocking is unneeded, all Pine trout are wild. From the west, steelhead and salmon are stopped from entering the Pine by a formidable barrier, Tippy Dam.

All who love the Pine can be thankful for the river clean-up efforts of the Traverse Area Paddle Club. The TAPC schedule not only several Pine efforts a year, but also river clean-ups on the Boardman, Jordan, AuSable, Sturgeon, & Betsie. If you'd like to join the TAPC, or assist them in their efforts, you can contact them through their website at www.traverseareapaddleclub.org.

The Pine meanders through an area of rich Michigan history, detailed in this book in a series of articles, including one about the most important day of fishing our country has ever known. Of all the joy that the Pine brings to us, it's biggest contribution to our lives began with one man fishing the river in 1925 near private land, an act that led to a lawsuit and a series of legal actions culminating in a *1936 Supreme Court decision confirming that anyone in the United States has the right to paddle or fish on a river – any river – through privately-owned land.*

To keep an ear on the Boys of Summer while paddling the Pine, turn your radio dial to 93.7FM. Go get 'em Tigers!

Paddle Now – Chores Later,
Doc

TUSTIN

The headwaters of the Pine River form 3.3 miles west of downtown Tustin, a small town of little more than 200 folks located in the northwestern portion of the Lower Peninsula. The village is 12 miles to the south of Cadillac and 1 mile east of US131. Driving into Tustin from the east provides a picturesque scene of barns and churches sitting among a series of rolling hills.

Tustin is on one of the highest points in the Lower Peninsula at an elevation of 1,233'. Looking west from downtown, the land slopes down until reaching the 1,102' elevation of where the Pine River's waters begin.

Near the Pine headwaters: the rolling hills of Tustin

Tustin was founded as a Swedish immigrant colony. Under the leadership of Reverend Josiah Tustin, one thousand Swedes immigrated to the west part of the state. In 1872, many of these pioneers settled in Tustin, originally called "New Bleking" in honor of the Swedish town of Blekinge, Sweden – although it was difficult to find any of the settlers who were actually from Blekinge. These immigrants formed the Swedish Evangelical Lutheran Church and since 1882 they've congregated in the building still in use today, on the south side of 20 Mile Road and just east of downtown.

The Swedish settlement of Tustin was the result of the meeting of two driving forces in the 1870s: (1) the desire of the railroad owners to build their business by developing the untouched wilderness of the northwestern Lower Peninsula and (2) the desire of Swedes to escape several years of near-starvation crop failures in Sweden. Advertising through the Swedish press and via stories spread by returning Swedes (among them the Reverend Josiah Tustin), the railroads offered a variety of incentives to those willing to emigrate to Michigan including: deferred transatlantic fares until the Swedes found employment here, free railroad transportation to Michigan from the immigrants arrival in New York, free settlement housing until a wage-earner could pay for their own house, and plenty of 40 acre parcels of land available at $5 an acre or through homesteading at $2.50 an acre.

Farming the rich land, cutting timber in the virgin forest, and taking jobs with the expanding railroads provided work for all who were looking. The crop yields were plentiful, unlike what the Swedes escaped back home. All of this nirvana took place in a climate very similar to their native Sweden. The extremely grateful settlers thanked the Reverend Josiah Tustin, in their eyes the man most responsible for bringing them to America, by changing the name of their new home from New Bleking to Tustin.

The 92-mile long White Pine Trail, running from Cadillac in the north to Grand Rapids in the south, passes through town alongside the Pine River Area Historical Society Museum, where much of Tustin's recorded history is displayed. The White Pine Trail is one of Michigan's "rail to trails" efforts & runs on the path originally graded for the Grand Rapids & Indiana Railroad. In 1994, the Michigan DNR took over of the property, removing the rails and transforming the old rail line into the trail that intersects Tustin today.

Tustin's Pine River Museum & part of the 92-mile long White Pine Trail

Winter on the Pine in the town of Riverbank

Logjam On The Pine & Wildlife Intentions and the town of Riverbank

Along the banks of the Pine, not far from the river's headwaters, surrounded by quiet, where no canoe & kayak livery operates, 3 paddling hours upstream from the easternmost public access of Edgetts, is the riverside rental cottage known as Logjam On The Pine. Next door is the Horan home and their enchanting art studio, Wildlife Intentions.

Logjam On The Pine & Wildlife Intentions are located in the very small town of Riverbank. According to a sign you pass as you drive into town, Riverbank was founded in 1910. The sign was painted by the man whose family owns the cottage and the art studio, Jerry Horan.

This Pine riverside property is owned by Jerry, Lori, and son Jeff Horan. Upstream from Logjam there are no public access sites and no vacation rentals, minimizing the chances of interruptions floating by the Logjam's peacefulness. The rustic Logjam cottage sleeps up to 8, a great place to relax after a day on the Pine whether you paddle a popular downstream section of the river or the remote stretch that runs through and beyond Riverbank (maybe a river trip with son Jeff as your guide). The riverside fire pit on the grounds allows you to wind down the day, comfortable by the campfire watching this beautiful river flow by.

A visit to Jerry's art studio, Wildlife Intentions, is as fun and as memorable as a night at Logjam. A canoe hangs over the front entrance to the studio. Inside is long paddle from a pole boat that once plied the AuSable River. As we slowly walked through his studio, soaking it all in, our main reaction was "wow!" Jerry's love of nature is on beautiful display through his creative works of art: wall-sized quilts, original acrylic art, & carvings of rainbow and brook trout, bald eagles, sandhill cranes, & Canadian geese created from driftwood found in the Pine River. The carvings of birds & fish seem to be trying to free themselves from the art studio walls, lamps, and tables they've been incorporated into.

Jerry began his career as a commercial artist for the Orlando (Florida) Daily News. Jerry's limited edition watercolor prints have received rave reviews from folks all over Michigan and beyond. Jerry once submitted one of his works for that year's Michigan state trout stamp – each year artists submit entries to compete for the right to be on the stamp – and among the many entries sent in, Jerry Horan's took 2nd place.

Outside of Logjam On The Pine & Wildlife Intentions, little remains of the town of Riverbank. In 1910, the Manistee & Grand Rapids Railroad ran a line through the area, connecting the towns of Marion and Manistee. The rail line ran east-west along the northern edge of the Horan's property, crossing over 17 Mile Road (the road that runs through Riverbank) a couple hundred yards west of the Logjam On The Pine. The 1st building you see looking east of Logjam was once the 1910-era cook shack for the railroad employees. The 2nd building west of Logjam was the early-1900s town post office & depot, and said to be where the son of Oliver Wendell Holmes once lived.

Once sawmill operators who utilized the waters of the Pine to float their logs closed up shop, the Manistee & Grand Rapids Railroad line through town stopped running and the general store closed. Today the town of Riverbank consists of Logjam On The Pine & Wildlife Intentions sitting alongside the banks of the sweetly meandering Pine River, and that folks, is an awful lot.

For more information go to www.logjamonthepine.com & www.jerryhoran.com or call (231) 829-3727. Take US131 to exit 168, follow east-west 20 Mile Rd west for 4 miles to Lakola Road and turn south (left). Take Lakola Rd south for 2 miles to the big left-hand turn on to 17 Mile Road (the only way you can go) and drive into Riverbank. Logjam will be on your left, just before crossing the Pine River.

Logjam on the Pine - a Jerry Horan carving

A Wildlife Intentions creation

Edgetts Lodge

The Pine viewed from Edgetts Lodge

Edgetts Lodge, a Lion Prowls the Riverbank, the Ghost Town of Edgetts

15 minutes upstream from the Pine River's first public access (the put-in downstream of Edgetts Bridge) is a 5,100 square foot rental property called Edgetts Lodge. Located on 38 wooded acres along the south bank of the Pine River, Edgetts Lodge is impressive from your first glimpse of its exterior as you drive in through the fine northern woods – and your experience is about to get even better. As soon as you enter the front door you're warmed by the rustic red pine beauty of the lodge. Most impressive is the view through the floor-to-ceiling picture windows of the Pine River flowing through the valley below. Edgetts Lodge is one of the finest among many sweet hideaways that we're blessed with here in Michigan.

Your Edgetts Lodge stay comes with the use of their 6 kayaks. Paddling one of these kayaks downstream from the lodge, you pass below Edgetts Bridge (Raymond Road). The 1st home on the left past the bridge is that of Dan and Janet LaRose. Dan was an offensive lineman for the Detroit Lions, starting for the team that had a very enjoyable 1962 Thanksgiving decisively handling Bart Starr & the great Green Bay Packer team by the score of 26 to 14. Dan is a member of the all-time University of Missouri football team, starred in the 1961 Orange Bowl (with JFK in attendance), and while in Missouri high school Dan set the state record for the shot put. As you paddle by Dan and Janet's Pine River log cabin home, look for his shot put pad in the backyard.

The ghost town of Edgetts was a prosperous late-1800s/early-1900s logging community and home to one of the stations of the Manistee & Grand Rapids Railroad. The rail line ran through the property of today's Edgetts Lodge. As late as the early-1920s, Edgetts was a fairly bustling town with a variety of businesses including a general store and a hotel – until a 1921 fire wiped out the entire village. On the adjacent page is a 1920 photo showing Edgetts before the fire, the view facing north from the Pine River on Raymond Road.

The address for Edgetts Lodge is 4944 N. Raymond Road, Luther MI 49656. For more information, go to www.edgettslodge.com or call (248) 894-5115. Take US131 to exit 168, follow east-west 20 Mile Road west for 5&1/2 miles to Raymond Road. Turn south (left) on Raymond Road and drive for 3 miles, crossing over the Pine River. Turn left at the 3rd drive south of the Pine, at the sign for "Huston/Slavsky". The lodge will be on your left.

The town of Edgetts in 1920, 1 year before the fire, looking
north from the Pine on Raymond Road - general store on
the left, hotel on the right (courtesy Doug Galloup)

PINE RIVER – DAY ONE

Edgetts to Skookum South
7.4 miles, 2 hours 30 minutes
Suggested Paddling Ability: Intermediate

River quote: Jake Leinenkugel "It takes a special beer to attract 25,000 men to a town with no women"

River quote 2: Kenny Q – "What do you call a deer with no eyes?" A- "No-I-D-Er"

Soundtrack: From the Beginning – Emerson, Lake, & Palmer; Will There Be Enough Water When My Ship Comes In? – The Dead Weather; And the Tide Rushes In – Moody Blues; Ghost Town – the Specials; The Journey – Adelaide

Directions to the launch site: from US131 exit 168 (Tustin) drive west on 20 Mile Road for 5 & 1/2 miles to Raymond Road and turn left (south). In 3 miles you will cross over the Pine. 1/10th of a mile before (north of) the river, turn right (west side of Raymond) on to the dirt road. This right hand turn is just north of the tin house. On the dirt road take the left fork to the river. Poison Ivy lines the walking path to the Pine, so stay on the path. The last 50' to the river takes you down a steep walkway.

Day One Overview: The Edgetts put-in is the furthest upstream access from which any Pine canoe & kayak livery will launch you from. It is 300' downstream from the Edgetts Road Bridge - where Raymond Road crosses over the river – and 43 miles upstream from the final public access (aka Norman Dixon) within in the Tippy Dam Pond. The Edgetts to Skookum South journey took our paddlers 2 & 1/2 hours in late-June, when water levels and the 3 mph current speed were considered "normal". Rapids greet you at the Edgetts launch site, with 12 additional exciting Day One rapids identified by our crack research team. This section of the Pine flows over multiple drops in the river floor, sudden dips ranging from 6" to 1' each. Between Edgetts and Skookum South, the river width will average 25', varying from 20' to 40', at a depth from 2' to 3'. You will frequently see rocks 3' to 4' in diameter covering the floor of the Pine, and plenty of merging feeder streams. Day One includes 3 additional access sites: Briar Patch (2 mile mark), Meadowbrook (3.5 miles), Skookum North (6.9 miles).

The 1 mile mark of the 43 mile long Pine River journey

Adyson – youngest member of the Crack Research Team

Day One in Miles and Minutes:

.3 miles/6 minutes: Light rapids takes you past the gorgeous creek merging from the right, loudly making its presence known, descending towards the river from stone to stone until it joins with the Pine.

.5 miles/10 minutes: House upon the left hill marks the spot where you should stay far left to avoid the large river rocks. Cedar trees line the shorelines.

.6 miles/13 minutes: Pine bends around a huge oxbow, taking you through some fine class 1 rapids wrapped around a huge midstream rock; frequent homes are visible beyond the left bank.

1 mile/22 minutes: Paddle beneath the clearly-marked "Phillips Bridge"; a sign upstream from the bridge lets you know that, in times of high water, squeezing below the bridge may be a problem. The riverbanks are frequently carpeted with beautiful fields of violet bluebell flowers.

1.4 miles/33 minutes: Pass by a midstream island with a great deal of wooded debris on its upstream end; easiest passage is to the island's right.

Rapids near Meadow Brook

1.9 miles/43 minutes: Very fun! A 30-second long rapids run through a rock garden kicks off intermittent whitewater over the next 5 minutes. Tag alder bushes line the shoreline.

2 miles/45 minutes: **Briar Patch access** is on the left bank, in the middle of the 5 minute long intermittent whitewater run. 4 minutes downstream you paddle beneath a pedestrian bridge.

2.7 miles/1 hour: Right bank private access precedes rapids flowing around and over some very large rocks.

3 miles/1 hour 6 minutes: Now we're talkin'! A sandy beach sits on the right at the start of a straightaway full of rapids and large rocks; the straightaway ends at a park bench atop a 50' tall ridge as the Pine bends left. This signals the start of a very enjoyable intermittent 8-minute run of class 1 and class 2 rapids; a sandy private access is on the right 6 minutes into the rapids.

3.5 miles/1 hour 17 minutes: **Meadowbrook access** is the narrow dirt path on the right, 50' before passing below 6 Mile Road Bridge. Big rocks/big rapids/ big fun! - this heralds the start of a windy and rocky 7 minutes of class 2 rapids, including a 1' gradient drop as the river wraps around an oxbow. Down from the rapids, the Pine widens to 40', the widest it will be today.

4 miles/1 hour 26 minutes: At a rock ledge is a 1' river drop; downstream wooden steps rising up the left bank precede a wooden fence atop the 25' tall left bank cliff.

4.2 miles/1 hour 30 minutes: Fine rapids take you over another rock ledge and 1' drop. Coe Creek, with great speed, merges right.

A Momma Merganser Duck & her babies

Excellent wildlife viewing: Momma and baby Merganser ducks are along the left riverbank; the crying screams of young river otters near the right shore create a very memorable sound.

4.5 miles/1 hour 37 minutes: Nice rapids flow beneath the left bank low leaning cedar trees. Over the next 3 minutes, you can feel the river floor drop below you as you traverse through 2 great rapids.

5 miles/1 hour 45 minutes: As the river bends left you see a 40' tall dirt hill on the right; 2 minutes downstream are dueling beaches, great break spots on both your right and left.

5.2 miles/1 hour 50 minutes: Log imbedded on the river floor creates a 6" drop.

6 miles/2 hours 4 minutes: Passing the home on the left with the brick lower-level and nice steps leading up from the Pine lets you know you're exactly 6 miles into today's trip. Rapids and a 6" river drop are seconds ahead.

6.2 miles/2 hours 8 minutes: Pass below the Skookum Road Bridge. Before the bridge are light rapids and on the right is the home with a long deck and cinder block lower level.

6.9 miles/2 hours 20 minutes: **Skookum Road North** access is on the right – nice, but a bit steeper and less user-friendly than Skookum South. 3 minutes downstream is a nice little 75' long rapids run, the last one today.

7.4 miles/2 hours 30 minutes: You are in! The **Skookum South** access is on the left.

The view upstream from the Skookum Road Bridge

The Edgetts to Skookum South Crack Research Team: Kenny Umphrey, Ethan Chandler Blake, Adyson Taylor Duckworth, Tommy Holbrook, Doc

HUNTING . . .

●

If you are interested in some of the finest Partridge, Rabbit or Deer shooting in the state, come up in the fall. Guides are furnished, and you are assured of good shooting.

·

Send in your Reservations Early as we can handle only a limited number.

·

OSCAR GALLOUP
Telephone Tustin 57-F13

R.F.D. 1   LUTHER, MICHIGAN

OSCAR'S
ON THE PINE

Excellent Fishing and Hunting

With a Comfortable Clean Farmhouse to Stay in

·

LUTHER, MICHIGAN

Back in the day...
(courtesy Doug Galloup)

15

PINE RIVER – DAY TWO

Skookum South to Walker
6.6 miles, 2 hours
Suggested Paddling Ability: Intermediate

River quote: JJ Johnson "A fartin' horse will never tire, a fartin' man's a man to hire"

River quote 2: Kenny "What's all over your face?" 5-yr old Adyson "Cookies!"

Soundtrack: Pure Michigan Statewide Sing-along; Deep River Blues – Doc Watson; Don't Fence Me In – David Byrne; In the Pines – Leadbelly; My Paddle's Keen and Bright – Margaret Embers McGee

Directions to the launch site: from US131 exit 168 (Tustin) drive 7 miles west on 20 Mile Road, which becomes 8 Mile Road in the town of Bristol. 7 miles west of US131, 8 Mile Rd bends sharply to the south (left) and becomes Skookum Road. Follow Skookum Road south for two miles to (shortly after crossing over the Pine River) 6 Mile Road. Turn west (right) on to 6 Mile Road. In 200' you reach Pine River Road – turn right and drive to the river access (to reach the Skookum North access: from Skookum South take 6 Mile Road east to Skookum Road and turn left/north; take first left north of the Pine).

Day Two Overview: Our crack research team explored Skookum South to Walker in late-June. Pine speed & depth were at their "normal" summertime levels, taking us 2 hours to travel the 6.6 miles as the Pine moved at 3.3 mph. The sand & stone riverbed averaged 2' deep & at times was as shallow as 6". The Pine's normal 30' width was occasionally narrowed to 10' openings by tag alder bushes leaning in from each bank. View 60' high banks with forests populated by birch and pine trees while paddling through long runs of rapids. The canoes and kayaks glide over 4' diameter rocks anchored on the Pine's floor.

6 of today's 6.6 miles flow through private land owned by a group referred to as the "Ne-Bo-Shone", a name with a Native American ring to it adopted by the landowners association. The public's right to paddle and fish this 6 mile section of the river, and thus through privately-owned land all across the US, was at the heart of a 1936 landmark US Supreme Court decision (for more details, read the chapter in this book entitled, "The Pine River, a Man Named Gideon, and the Most Important Day of Fishing Our Country Has Ever Known").

Day Two in Miles and Minutes:

.2 miles/5 minutes: 50' into the woods on the left, a sign announces your entry into the property of the "Ne-Bo-Shone". Soon pass a large sign on the right shore reading "Notice – private property/next 6 miles to Walker Bridge (2 hours)/No trespassing – patrolled/ Ne-Bo-Shone Association". Just downstream is a sweet 200' long set of riffles running over river floor rocks 2' to 3' in diameter.

Entering Ne-Bo-Shone property

.6 miles/13 minutes: Paddle alongside fields of fern and stands of birch; once around the oxbow/peninsula you see to the left the first Ne-Bo-Shone home.

1 mile/20 minutes: Shallow and gorgeous rapids flow beneath the green footbridge labeled "Ne-Bo-Shone"; homes are now visible on both sides of the Pine, many circa 1920s in appearance (Tom noted the homes are "not over the top – they look comfortable"). The Pine soon flows over river floor rocks as large as manatees; the river depth is 2' with occasional deeper holes stepping off underwater clay ledges.

2 miles/38 minutes: An exciting run begins! Over the next 17 minutes you paddle through intermittent rapids wrapped around large rocks. The Pine never looked more beautiful. As an added treat, a Momma Merganser duck and her 9 babies dart below bushes near the shoreline.

2.4 miles/46 minutes: Along the right bank, ancient pilings jut just above water line. 4 minutes downstream, a home and deck tower 80' above us on the right, preceding a fetching tiny creek merging right.

2.9 miles/55 minutes: The 17-minute long rapids run comes to a glorious conclusion; on one of the tall pines beyond the right shore is a sign reminding us that we're paddling alongside Ne-Bo-Shone property. In 2 minutes, paddle below a pedestrian bridge supported by stone columns; a water depth gauge is just past the bridge, on the left.

3.2 miles/1 hour: 60-second long rapids run winds around 2 midstream rocks jutting barely above the river surface, lined up one 50' after the other. At the end of a straightaway and on your right is a gorgeous stand of pine trees that follows the river as it bends left; downstream are banks of clay visible up to 3' above the waterline.

3.5 miles/1 hour 7 minutes: At a right bend of the river & on the left bank is a fine looking 2-story Pine home with a huge balcony; a few feet beyond is a midstream island passable right or left. Cedar trees lean in from the right.

4 miles/1 hour 15 minutes: Winding around two bends is a great rapids run flowing around large midstream rocks.

4.2 miles/1 hour 20 minutes: From the left, a small tributary flows beneath a concrete bridge before it empties into the Pine. 3 minutes downstream, rapids take you below a footbridge. A 2-tiered sandy beach is on the right.

Day 2 bridge, 3 miles from launch

Rapids 4 miles downstream from Skookum South

4.6 miles/1 hour 26 minutes: A creek merges from the right; looking up the creek, visible in the distance is a home on a hill. One minute later, paddle through a lovely little riffle run.

4.9 miles/1 hour 30 minutes: The house with many windows sits high on a ridge beyond the right bank. The Pine creates an oxbow as it winds left. The riverbed is 50' wide and 1' deep as it flows by a field of ferns on the left.

5.5 miles/1 hour 40 minutes: At a right bend, the river flows around a midstream island with a stone and sand beach; light rapids follow. Blue herons are flying ahead. 5 minutes downstream, an abandoned small structure with a stone chimney is on the right.

5.9 miles/1 hour 46 minutes: Paddle beneath the State Road Bridge and a smaller bridge a few feet ahead: This is the end of the Ne-Bo-Shone Association property. Between the 2, on the left and above the wooden seawall, is the "Walker Bridge Canoe Livery", the only livery located on the banks of the Pine (spelled out in large letters at the livery is C-A-N-O-E-I-N-G). Very nice homes line the riverbank beyond the two bridges.

6.2 miles/1 hour 50 minutes: A dirt access is on the right, running down to the river through an opening in the wooden fence that runs parallel to the Pine. You are now paddling through the Silver Creek Campground on your right. Very enjoyable light rapids run alongside the campground. A second access, with stairs leading down to the river, is 5 minutes after the dirt access and also on the right.

6.6 miles/2 hours: You are in! The **Walker Bridge** access is at the steps on the right (the 3rd Silver Creek Campground access you come to). 50' past the access is a wooden footbridge with the sign "low clearance".

The Skookum South to Walker Bridge Crack Research Team: JJ Johnson, Kenny Umphrey, Ethan Chandler Blake, Adyson Taylor Duckworth, Tommy Holbrook, Doc

Day 2 ends at the Walker Access

The Pine River, a Man Named Gideon, and the Most Important Day of Fishing Our Country Has Ever Known

The years of 1935 and 1936 were fabulous ones for Michigan sports enthusiasts...

- The Detroit Tigers win their 1st World Series title in '35 when Goose Goslin's single scores Mickey Cochrane with the winning run in Game 6 against the Chicago Cubs.
- The Detroit Lions, led by quarterback Dutch Clark, defeat the NY Giants in 1935 & win their 1st National Football League Championship.
- The Detroit Red Wings win their 1st Stanley Cup, eliminating the Toronto Maple Leafs in the 1935-'36 Finals.
- In a boxing ring set up in Yankee Stadium in 1935, Detroit's "Brown Bomber", Joe Louis, out-boxes Max Baer (Jethro Bodine's father – it all comes back to the Beverly Hillbillies, doesn't it?).

All of these were moments of huge happiness for Michigan folks, but the victory that brought the longest-lasting joy, not only to sports lovers in Michigan, but to those all across the country, was a 1936 victory often over-looked today. This victory was won by one man, knowing he was in the right, and his determination not to be beaten by big money.

This victory started in the middle of the Pine River.

In May of 1925, Gideon Gerhardt began the most important day of fishin' that our country has ever known. He was trout fishing on the Pine, west of Skookum Road. As Gideon waded further downstream, he came upon barbed wire strung from shore to shore, with "No Fishing" signs placed nearby. The barbed wire and the signs were placed there by a wealthy man who owned 120 riverside acres, an Ohioan named Frank Collins.

Gideon believed that it was his right to fish anywhere he wanted to in the Pine because (1) the Pine had *always* been opened for everyone to use, even before the logging days of the 1800s, and (2) the Pine had been stocked with four and one-half million trout by the State Conservation Department – the cost of this paid for by fees charged to Michigan's anglers.

So, Gideon Gerhardt climbed over the barbed wire – and Frank Collins sued him for trespassing.

The local justice of the peace found in Gerhardt's favor. Collins appealed to the Lake County Circuit Court, where Gerhardt again won yet was fined six cents in damages. Although only a nominal fine, Gerhardt felt that on principal this was wrong, and – to the benefit of all who love to paddle & fish our rivers - appealed to the Michigan Supreme Court. The Michigan Supreme Court, citing a 1787 ordinance that covered territory including what is today Michigan, determined all navigable waterways and the soil beneath them were held in a trust for the use of the people AND that, since the Pine had once been used to float logs, the river met the criteria to be considered a navigable waterway. The court also made Collins pay Gerhardt his six cent fine back.

The Michigan Supreme Court decision also stated that this right of all to the river did not extend to adjacent privately-owned riverbanks, i.e. the public could use any part of the river, but could not trespass on shore. Frank Collins used this part of the court's decision to his benefit: Frank and the Ne-Bo-Shone Association, an Ohio-based group of which he was a member, purchased almost 8 continuous miles of land along the Pine River – a distance too long for most fishermen to wade. You could still paddle and float this stretch of the river, but canoers soon reported the building of enormous logjams, harassment by armed guards from land, even pointed stakes buried in the river floor that ripped open canoes floating above.

In 1932, Frank Collins and the Ne-Bo-Shone Association were ordered by the state to remove their barriers and restore the navigability of the Pine River. The Ne-Bo-Shone petitioned the U.S. Court of Appeals, who ruled against them in 1934, and then to the United States Supreme Court, who decided in 1936 to refuse the group a new hearing. It was 1936 after all – Michigan was destined to win.

Due to the actions of one man on the Pine River, canoers and kayakers in the USA may paddle down a river through privately-owned land with the law firmly on their side. The results of the action taken by Gideon Gerhardt on a May day in 1925 are recognized along the Pine at Peterson's Landing, just upstream from the M37 Bridge: in 1988, a Michigan Legal Milestone marker was placed here, commemorating one of the most important water-rights decision in the history of our country. The next time you visit the marker, it might be a nice touch to leave six cents in Gideon's name.

Due to the actions of one man on the Pine River, canoers and kayakers in the USA may paddle down a river through privately-owned land with the law firmly on their side.

Downstream view from the Walker Bridge

PINE RIVER – DAY THREE

Walker to Dobson
12.1 miles, 3 hours
Suggested Paddling Ability: Intermediate

River quote: Maggie "All in all, I like my princess lifestyle – just to be clear, that does not include paddling in this weather"

River quote 2: Doc "I chilled my hiney on the Piney"

Soundtrack: Sea of Madness – Crosby, Stills, Nash & Young; Cool Water – Sons of the Pioneers; Ride Captain Ride – Blues Image; Frederic Chopin – Impromptu No. 1 in A Flat; Willow Weep For Me – Billie Holiday

Directions to the launch site: from US131 exit 168 (Tustin) drive 6 miles west on 20 Mile Road, which becomes 8 Mile Road in the town of Bristol. 2 miles after passing through Bristol (i.e. 2 miles past the gas station at Raymond Road) turn north (right) on to Sadler Road. Take this dirt road north for 1 mile to 9 Mile Road and turn west (left). Follow 9 Mile Road until it ends at State Road. Turn south (left) on to State and in about one minute the access at the Walker Bridge Canoe Livery will be on your right.

Day Three Overview: A bit nippy it was as our crack research team paddled the Pine from Walker to the Dobson Bridge access in 35 degree, early- May weather. The fast current was bolstered by the high springtime water level as we motored through the 12 miles at 4 mph (Walker-Dobson is usually considered a 4-hour run). The depth averages 4' and width 30' as you paddle alongside tall cliffs of birch, cedar, and pine. Good steering skills are needed to maneuver through and around class 1 rapids, midstream boulders, and occasional debris fields.

2.5 miles into today's trip takes you by the Lincoln access, the starting point for the last 26 miles of the river, a section of the Pine designated in 1992 as a "National and Scenic River". Arriving at the Elm Flats public access, 5.5 miles downstream from today's Walker access launch, you enter the Huron-Manistee National Forest, the start of the "permitted" portion of the Pine: from Memorial Day Friday through Labor Day, every water craft requires a daily permit, available at www.recreation.gov (additional info at the Manistee Ranger Station 231-723-2211).

Waiting to launch at the Walker access

Day Three in Miles and Minutes:

Depart from the downstream end of the Silver Creek Campground. 50' from launch pass beneath a wooden footbridge displaying a "low clearance" sign.

.9 miles/13 minutes: Cedar trees lean towards the river from the right bank, forming a right-of-midstream canopy. In 2 minutes, at today's 1 mile mark, a stream flows down a right bank hill as the Pine bends left. For the next 3 minutes wind your way through fun rapids flowing over large rocks just below the river surface. As the rapids end, pass by a long field of trillium flowers on the right.

2.1 miles/32 minutes: Two side-by-side creeks merge from the left and precede a fine 2-minute long rapids run. In 5 minutes, 2.5 miles from launch, the **Lincoln access** landing is on the right.

2.7 miles/40 minutes: Beautiful creek rolls in from the right; ahead is a very enjoyable 2-minutes long rapids run. 3 minutes beyond these rapids, next to a 20' long midstream island, is a sandy beach on the right shore.

3.8 miles/54 minutes: Beneath the hardwoods atop the high cliff, a creek merges into the Pine from the left; 2 minutes later, a creek winds down a hill from your right. In 4 minutes, pass by back-to-back sandy beaches, first right shore – across from a 70' tall cliff - then left.

4.3 miles/1 hour: Huge debris field blocks all but 10' along the left bank. 8 minutes downstream, a 2nd huge debris field, backing up to a sandy island, is passable only on the left.

5.3 miles/1 hour 14 minutes: As river bends left, you see a small green structure beyond the right bank. In 2 minutes, the **Elm Flats access** is on the right. A sign at the landing announces you're "entering Huron-Manistee Forest next 23 miles – no camping within 1/4 mile of the river".

6.3 miles/1 hour 32 minutes: Sandy beach break spot at a left river bend. There are frequent mallards sightings. 2 minutes downstream is an island with passage on the left, obstructions blocking the right, and light rapids visible ahead. A great deal of beaver activity is evident just beyond the river's edge.

6.9 miles/1 hour 37 minutes: 15' long sandy beach on the right; 6 minutes downstream, among spectacular cedars and birch trees, is another right shore sandy beach.

7.5 miles/1 hour 52 minutes: Fast-flowing Popular Creek flows into the Pine from your right, one minute before you're into a fine whitewater run.

7.8 miles/1 hour 56 minutes: *Challenging rapids run!* The Pine wraps around a peninsula where a brown home and deck sit. Just downstream is a fabulous 2 minutes through today's most exciting rapids, featuring boulders both left and right of midstream, and requiring skilled steering.

8.3 miles/2 hours 6 minutes: Very fun 3-minute long rapids take you over & around multiple fallen trees and large rocks inches below the surface. 7 minutes downstream, the 30' long sandy beach on the right makes an excellent break spot. Continue 3 minutes to a similarly good break spot at the left of center 50' long island.

9.4 miles/2 hours 20 minutes: Nice rapids, but be aware of the large boulder in the middle of them. In 3 minutes, 15' high overlooking the river, sits a fine home and deck.

10 miles/2 hour 27 minutes: Right bank sandy break area is across the Pine from log cabin atop a 20' embankment. Impressive beaver activity is visible. A good looking weeping willow is 3 minutes downstream.

10.5 miles/2 hours 35 minutes: At left bend, 60' cliff is across the river from another sandy beach. In one more paddling minute, a gorgeous field of trillium flowers carpets the right bank. 10 minutes downstream, as the Pine turns left, a stream flows down a right bank hill.

11.4 miles/2 hours 48 minutes: Pass below telephone lines; left of midstream is a huge rock embedded in the river floor, 6" above the waterline (during spring high water conditions). 150' beyond is a sandy break spot on the left.

11.8 miles/2 hours 55 minutes: A beautiful left bank log-cabin style home with adjacent 3-season enclosure sits atop a wooden seawall. Upstream from Dobson Bridge and on the right is an A-frame with chalet-style guest homes.

12.1 miles/3 hours: You are in! Paddle through the rapids beneath Dobson Bridge and take-out at the **Dobson access** on the right.

The Walker to Dobson Bridge Crack Research Team: Clan Braun members Colonel, Julie, Eric aka Milford Slim, Karen, and (holding down the fort) Big Joe, along with Maggie and Doc

River Songs sung by Clan Braun

Our Sad Loss: the Grayling
gone with the michigan that once was

The Michigan Grayling

"Doubtless God could make a better fish than the Michigan grayling but doubtless He never did" William B. Mershon

From just before the 1840s and up until the 1880s there was only one game fish in the Pine River and in the entire watersheds of the Manistee and the AuSable Rivers. This beautiful fish, recognized by its slate blue color and sail-like dorsal fin, identified and formally named in 1865, native to Michigan, the namesake of one of the state's northern towns, known to be abundant, said to be delicious, and now extinct, is the Michigan grayling.

The Michigan grayling was last seen in the Lower Peninsula in the 1910s and in the Upper Peninsula in the 1930s. The last known grayling to be caught was in 1937 by Robert Smock Sr. and is believed to be mounted and on display in a DNR office somewhere in Michigan.

The Michigan grayling fell prey to overfishing, the destruction of its habitat during the logging days of the late-1800s/early-1900s, and the introduction of aggressive non-native trout to our waters…

- Fishing limits did not exist in the 1800s and back then grayling were taken home by the wagon-full.

- Logging removed tall trees that shaded the Pine and other rivers, making their waters too warm for the cold-water loving grayling; the felled cut trees created logjams, decimating grayling spawning areas.

- The grayling did not have to compete with brown trout until 1884, the year that trout eggs were first planted into a United States river (the Pere Marquette) as a gift from their native Germany.

Michigan was the only Midwestern home of the grayling, a fish still found today in western wilderness areas of USA and Canada. The DNR attempted to reintroduce the grayling to Michigan waters by planting them into the AuSable River near Mio. Brown trout were the prime beneficiary of this effort as it was in their stomachs that most of these graylings ended up.

Some believe that a few Michigan grayling may still exist. On the state's DNR website is posted this: *Anglers – chances are very remote that you will ever catch a grayling in Michigan, but if you do, you must return it to the water immediately!*

Spring logjam

Beneath the Hoxeyville High Bridge

PINE RIVER – DAY FOUR

Dobson to Peterson
6.3 miles, 1 hour 33 minutes
Suggested Paddling Ability: Intermediate/Skilled

River quote: Kenny (as he careened into the riverbank) "I couldn't see – I was talking"

River quote 2: Doc "Plan thoroughly, but be prepared to follow the current"

Soundtrack: I've Got Sand In My Shoes – the Drifters; Look Into the Sun – Jethro Tull; Sea of Joy – Blind Faith; Deadwood – Mountain Heart; If The Sea Was Whiskey – Willie Dixon

Directions to the launch site: from the M55 and M37 junction, take M37 south (crossing over the Pine) for 2.5 miles. Turn east (left) at W 48&1/2 Road (Kestelwoods Restaurant at corner). Drive 2.2 miles on W 48&1/2 Road, cross over the Pine on Dobson Bridge and turn left.

Just east of Dobson Bridge is a car spotting service: 231-862-3480.

Day Four Overview: Our crack research team paddled two canoes down this stretch of the Pine in gorgeous late-April weather. The Pine is always fast between Dobson and Peterson, just a tick more so in the higher springtime water levels we encountered (as contrast, in late-August low water, Dobson to Peterson took us 1 hour 50 minutes to paddle: 17 minutes longer than today).

On this journey you paddle through delightfully challenging rapids, by sandy cliffs and sand beaches, and enjoy excellent wildlife viewing including wood ducks, mergansers, hawks and beavers. Shorelines are often covered with a thick forest of hardwoods. On this stretch of the Pine, the river averages 30' in width and 2' to 3' deep.

There is also a campground along the ride: 30 minutes downstream from the Dobson access you'll pass by the Coolwater Campground on the left shore.

Day Four in Miles and Minutes:

.5 mile/8 minutes: At the one-half mile mark are the first homes of the day, both on the left; there is a 70' tall ridge at the end of the straightaway; the surrounding woods are full of cedar, birch, and pine.

In the early going there are frequent riffles – no rapids yet, a series of right bank ridges, several sandy beaches, and quite a few mergansers and wood ducks.

1.2 miles/19 minutes: A pretty scene and a nice break spot – at a right river bend is a sandy beach on the left & just beyond and left a picturesque cliff; a red-headed woodpecker is nearby.

1.7 miles/27 minutes: The access for Coolwater Campground is on your left.

2.2 miles/35 minutes: On a sandy hill, at a right bend on the Pine, are the hillside holes of a bird sanctuary; at the base of fallen trees, all signs point to an active local beaver community. 3 minutes downstream and at the end of a straightaway you see a deck on a 60' tall ridge, giving the owner a sweeping view of the Pine River valley below.

2.5 miles/40 minutes: Pass beneath the Hoxeyville High Bridge; a few feet beyond are the first rapids today, running for a full minute (1/10ᵗʰ of a mile) & concluding at the end of a straightaway where a gorgeous log cabin home with a stone chimney sits on the left bank as the Pine bends right.

Past the log cabin home, the rapids quickly resume, brief but excellent class 2s, an 80' long run.

2.9 miles/50 minutes: Paddle through a series of light class 1 rapids for the next two minutes. The river here is only 6" deep and 30' wide. 3 hawks are circling above.

3.3 miles/53 minutes: All on your right... steps rise from the river up to the top of a 40' tall hill, where there's a wood home and fence. Just beyond is a loud and pretty waterfall, its last 2' visible as it emerges from the forest. Past the waterfall, light rapids dissolve into pleasant riffles.

3.5 miles/58 minutes: At a left river bend, a fine beach is directly across the river from a 70' tall cliff; at the next bend, an even taller cliff is across from another nice beach.

3.8 miles/1 hour: Light rapids take you past a beautiful wooden home on the left shore.

4 miles/1 hour 3 minutes: An excellent two-minute set of rapids begins.

4.3 miles/1 hour 8 minutes: The sandy beach on the right precedes brief rapids.

View from Dobson-Peterson bluff

Running a 6-minute long rapids

4.5 miles/1 hour 10 minutes: Outstanding rapids over the next 6 minutes! Kicks off where the Pine is 6" deep and the river turns left, launching you into a gorgeous stretch of fast water running the entire length of a 500' long straightaway, wrapping around the next bend. After a brief spell of flat water, the river rockets off again, turning left and passing a midstream island that narrows the river, intensifying the speed of the rapids. These are healthy class 1s, borderline class 2s. 6 minutes after starting up, the rapids end at a sandy beach and then briefly resume just beyond.

5.2 miles/1 hour 20 minutes: Biggest beach of the day comes into view on the left bank, right after the Pine turns left; delightful class 1s begin in front of this beach and will run on and off for the next 8 minutes. A real treat!

6 miles/1 hour 30 minutes: On a high ridge right is a fence, the first sign of the Peterson Landing; you'll then see steps rise up a left bank. You are now paddling through a fine stretch of class 1s that will take you to today's end; pass by the left bank take-out for Peterson's Campground (across the river from the landing). The sign says keep right 500' for the landing.

6.3 miles/1 hour 33 minutes: You are in! **Peterson Landing** is on the right.

The Dobson to Peterson Crack Research Team: Paul "Mister P" Pienta, Juan Shell, Kenny Umphrey, and Doc

PINE RIVER – DAY FIVE

Peterson to Low Bridge
8.7 miles, 2 hour 12 minutes
Suggested Paddling Ability: Skilled

River quote: Chris "Is this heaven?" Kenny "Yes it is"

River quote 2: while looking over the Peterson Landing rapids, Kenny asked canoeing partner Shawn "You are a swimmer, right?"

Soundtrack: Michigan Water Blues – Jelly Roll Morton; Rednecks, White Socks and Blue Ribbon Beer – Johnny Russell; Pump It Up – Elvis Costello; Rondo alla Turca – Mozart; Pearl of the Quarter – Steely Dan

Directions to the launch site: from the M55 and M37 junction, take M37 south for 1.5 miles. Just before crossing over the Pine River, turn to the east (left). The landing is on the river's north bank (the U.S. Forest Service Campground is across the river, on its south bank).

Day Five Overview: Our crack research team canoed and kayaked down this stretch of the Pine in late-April. Due to the higher springtime river levels, the time listed here may be faster than what you will experience during a summertime paddle (Peterson to Low is frequently considered to be a 3 hour paddle).

Within the Peterson to Low Bridge stretch of the Pine is the fastest water of the entire river. Except for 30 minutes of calm between the 5 mile and 7 mile marks, you'll enjoy a full day of class 1 and 2 rapids, with few breaks between. This is not a safe section of the Pine for beginners, but it is a thrill for experienced paddlers. Although fast throughout today's 8.7 miles (as the Pine descends 101', or 11.6' per mile), the river is particularly exhilarating from the one-half mile mark (10 minutes from launch) to the 1 mile mark, a five-minute downhill run that will bring you back time and time again.

Peterson to Low gives you plenty of opportunities to pull over, stretch your legs, and get your voice back from all of the happy shouts: crack researchers counted an astounding 60 fine sandy break spots along today's trip. Wow!

As you paddle alongside forests of pines, cedars, willows, and birch, you are paddling through a riverbed averaging 2' deep and 30' wide.

Day 5 Peterson launch

M37 Bridge ahead

Pine viewed upstream from the M37 Bridge

Pine downstream from M37 Bridge

Pine in winter, downstream from M37 Bridge

Day Five in Miles and Minutes:

.1 mile/3 minutes: Rapids take you beneath the north/south M37 Bridge. Downstream, a long 80' tall sand dune is on the right.

.5 mile/10 minutes: ***5 minutes (one-half mile) of spectacular and almost continuous rapids!*** The starting point is the 1/10th mile long straightaway ending at a gorgeous log home sitting on a high ridge. This wild 5-minute ride, featuring class 1 and 2 rapids, ends at the 1 mile mark. Our GPS tells us that the river floor descends an amazing 20' over today's first mile.

The Fabulous Peterson Rapids

1.2 miles/18 minutes: Huge midstream tree trunk sticks 3' above the water line; on the left is a 100' tall sandy bank.

1.5 miles/23 minutes: River bends hard right concluding a fine set of rapids. An excellent sandy break spot with a beautiful cedar tree on the right sits across the Pine from a hillside waterfall. Immediately beyond this beach, the river picks up speed again and you are rocketed down a long straightaway of class 2 rapids. Treat yourself to a fabulous elevated view of these rapids (see page vi photo near the front of the book) by pulling over at the right point sandy beach, and walking downstream up the rise along the Pine. Bring your camera!

2.3 miles/34 minutes: Two exciting bends of rapids end as a sandy beach, across from a forest of cedar trees, wraps around a right river turn.

2.9 miles/43 minutes: At a left river bend is a beautifully long sandy beach. Two minutes downstream, the mirror-image of this beach is on the right. We're paddling alongside river otters.

3.7 miles/56 minutes: Over 3 minutes are two fantastic whitewater runs with a short respite between the two; the 3 minutes end at a right shore beach. One minute beyond the beach, pass by a large midstream island.

4.8 miles/1 hour 14 minutes: Rapids wrap around two back-to-back midstream islands; in two minutes class 1 rapids take you by a 120' tall left bend ridge.

5 miles/1 hour 18 minutes: Great pullover spot on the right point. Two minutes beyond, paddle by a 130' cliff on the right, the tallest seen today.

During the next 30 minutes, from the 5 mile mark to the 7 mile mark, there will be no rapids, only occasional riffles.

5.4 miles/1 hour 25 minutes: After the right bend is a 30' long sandy beach; in 3 paddling minutes, dueling sandy beaches face each other across the Pine.

7 miles/1 hour 47 minutes: At the end of a short straightaway is a beach and a house atop a 60' tall hill; over the next 4 minutes, paddle through a series of light & enjoyable class 1s ending at a 100' tall bluff covered with birch.

7.5 miles/1 hour 54 minutes: 150' long stone and dirt beach on the right extends out into the Pine, narrowing the river and creating rapids; ahead on the left is another beach.

7.7 miles/1 hour 56 minutes: Stay to the right as the river floor takes a big midstream drop.

8.7 miles/2 hours 12 minutes: You are in! The **Low Bridge** access is on the left.

The Peterson to Low Bridge Crack Research Team: Keith "Jonesey" Jones, Paul "Mister P" Pienta, Kenny Umphrey, Vid Marvin, Chris Weaks, Juan Shell, Shawn Kearney, Rob McCormick, Doc

5 miles downstream from the Peterson launch: the tallest cliff on Day 5

Just upstream from the Low Bridge access

Wellston and the Historic Wellston Inn

On the south side of M55, 20 miles east of the Lake Michigan shoreline community of Manistee, and about a 5-minute drive southeast of where the Pine River comes to an end in the Tippy Dam Pond, is the town of Wellston.

Alongside the railroad bed of the Chicago and West Michigan Railroad Co., the Swigart Land Co. founded Wellston in 1885. Wellston's post office opened in 1892, the town named after its first postmaster, Adelmer J. Wells. In the late-1800s, the railroad company promoted the region as a fisherman's and a hunter's paradise: Wellston is located in the Manistee National Forest and, in addition to the Pine and Tippy Dam Pond, within 5 miles of the town are 9 lakes and a stretch of the Manistee River, making Wellston a great canoeing, kayaking, big boat, and fishing destination.

One of Wellston's greatest treasures is also one of Michigan's: the Historic Wellston Inn. After a day or a week of paddling down the Pine, enjoying a meal within the golden knotty pine walls of the Inn, only steps away from a comfortable bed, provides an excellent ending to a great river adventure. In 1896, the "Hotel Wellston" opened to folks visiting the area. In 1900, the Swigart Land Co. built a real estate office next door - what today is the motel. Along with adjacent buildings constructed since the early 1900s, the Wellston Inn sleeps 88 in its 6 motel rooms, 4 cabins and the original lodge. At various times since its 1896 opening, besides providing beds and meals, the lodge has served as a church, a courthouse, and a community center.

A 1930's newspaper article posted in the Inn could have been written today: "Wellston – the home of good fishing... soul easing surroundings... you'll awake each morning with a spirit of renewed energy, happy and ready for play".

At the end of the 2000s, the Wellston Inn sat closed for 3 years – but then a town native who is a bundle of energy returned home and brought the Inn back to life. Colleen Sexton's studies and career took her away from Wellston, including an 8-year stint with the Coast Guard, serving time as a corrections officer, and opening and running a successful restaurant – successful enough that a local bank agreed to give Colleen a lease on the Inn.

Colleen held the Inn's grand opening on October 13, 2012, a day celebrated by both local folks and tourists, all with their own special memories of a century-worth of great times at the Inn with friends, spouses, kids, parents, and grandparents.

The Historic Wellston Inn is located on Seaman Road one mile south of M55. Their address is 17204 6th Street in Wellston, MI 49689; the Inn's phone number is 231-848-7102.

Early-1900s at the Wellston Inn (courtesy Wellston Inn)

Wellston in 1913 (courtesy Wellston Inn)

Little Mary's Hospitality House in Wellston

Trumping the physical beauty of the Wellston area – quite a feat - is the beauty of the spiritual gift that is Little Mary's Hospitality House...

Mary Fischer was just 3 years old when she was lost to a brain tumor in 1982. Tom and Maureen decided to honor their daughter's life by helping families with children who have illnesses from debilitating to terminal. To lend this helping hand, the Fischers opened "Little Mary's Hospitality House" the same year that their daughter left them.

Little Mary's sits on the edge of Crystal Lake in Wellston. The House has 6 private apartments, each with their own special theme, to create a fun, vacation feel. The themes are Country, Fantasyland, Mexico, Northern Michigan, Safari, and Western. Thousands of families from all over the world have traveled to Wellston for a stay at Little Mary's where terminally-ill adults and families who've previously lost a child to an illness are also welcome guests.

Each of the 6 apartments sleeps 6 to 8 (in 2 large bedrooms) and comes with their own kitchen, a private bath, and large living room – and all stays are free of charge. Little Mary's recreational center includes a non-denominational chapel, a game room, a library, a reflection room, and an outdoor playground with a fort, swing sets, a basketball court, a mini-Mackinaw Bridge, and beautiful wooden carvings. Canoeing, swimming, fishing, and boating are water activities offered, and guests may participate in group activities like nightly campfires, horseback riding, and family potlucks.

On the Little Mary's website, www.littlemarys.org, is a documentary with the heart-warming story of the Fischer family's 1982 World's Fair vacation, their last with their Mary, the vacation that served as the inspiration to open the Hospitality House. Little Mary's Hospitality House is located at 1580 Seaman Road in Wellston 49689, one mile south of M55. Their phone number is (231) 848-4699.

The Pine River Expedition Crew aka the Crack Research Team
by the Norman-Dixon access at Tippy Dam Pond

PINE RIVER – DAY SIX

Low Bridge to Tippy Dam Pond
2.2 miles, 50 minutes
Suggested Paddling Ability: Beginner

River quote: Vid "There's more than one Pine River"

River quote 2: Jim Horina "I'm so happy its spring. I was tired of wearing shoes and socks"

Soundtrack: Into the Mystic – Van Morrison; Summer Samba – Billy May; When the Levee Breaks – Led Zeppelin; Goin Down Slow – Lightnin' Hopkins; Especially in Michigan – Red Hot Chili Peppers

Directions to the launch site: from the M55 and M37 junction, take M55 west (towards Wellston & Manistee) for 4 & 1/2 miles to the Roadside Park on the south (left) side of M55. Go south for 1/2 mile to the access.

To today's end point, the Norman-Dixon Landing at Tippy Dam Pond, from the M55/M37 junction take M55 west 6 miles to Snyder Road and turn north (right). Take Snyder north for 1 & 1/2 miles to Robinson Road (at "Tippy Pond Boat Ramp" sign) and turn east (right). Go 1/2 mile to the boat ramp.

Day Six Overview: Our crack research team paddled this last leg of the Pine in late-April. The Pine was at higher springtime levels with the mild current slightly faster than summertime speed. During late-summer low-water, as the river empties into Tippy Pond (1.6 miles from launch), there may be bottom-scraping at the edge of the pond.

Approaching the M55 Bridge

Vid's comment that "there's more than one Pine" referred to the dramatic difference between today's journey and the previous 41 miles (from Edgetts to Low Bridge). Low Bridge to Tippy Dam Pond is a laidback float through flat water, with none of the rapids experienced during the Pine's first 5 days.

Today you'll enjoy paddling beneath the tall M55 Bridge, around a series of midstream sandy islands, through an area thick with pine and birch trees. At the end of today's trip camping is available: directly across Tippy Dam Pond from the Norman-Dixon landing, is USFS Camp Site 41, a paddle-in/boat-in only site with room for up to 40 tents (a primitive, poorly marked location, discovered through the tireless reconnaissance of the crack research team).

Both the Pine River and the Manistee River flow into Tippy Dam Pond, the Pine entering from the southeast and the Manistee from the northeast. The pond is where the Pine comes to an end, absorbed by the Manistee River as it exits the pond and continues its westward flow towards Lake Michigan.

Day Six in Miles and Minutes:

Launching at the Low Bridge access, the Pine is flat water, 70' wide, and 2' deep. Within 2 minutes, paddle under the Low Bridge.

.7 miles/14 minutes: Paddle beneath the high bridge at M55; below the bridge is a beautiful walkway on its east side (to your right).

The Pine flowing left to right below the M55 Bridge

Upstream view from the M55 Bridge

Downstream view from the M55 Bridge

After passing beneath the bridge, the Pine takes you into a long, northbound straightaway past a series of islands. There is a great elevated view of this section of the Pine from the pedestrian walkway on the north side of M55.

1.1 miles/23 minutes: Reach the end of the straightaway at a long, sandy beach island. Follow the river as it veers to the left (paddling right takes you into a backwater alcove).

1.4 miles/29 minutes: Begin to paddle alongside several sandy islands that make excellent break or picnic spots.

1.6 miles/34 minutes: Reach the southeastern edge of Tippy Pond; on the right shore is the Loomis Landing Campground & Marina with ten dock slips.

The Pine comes to an end: the Norman-Dixon landing at Tippy Dam Pond

2.2 miles/50 minutes: You are in! The **Norman-Dixon** boat ramp access is tucked into an alcove on the left bank.

The Low Bridge to Norman-Dixon Crack Research Team: Keith "Jonesey" Jones, Paul "Mister P" Pienta, Kenny Umphrey, Vid Marvin, Chris Weaks, Laz Surabian, Shawn Kearney, Rob McCormick, John Steck, D

PINE RIVER TAVERN: MINERAL SPRINGS PIZZA PUB AND GRILL

Near the Pine's headwaters is a fine tavern to kick back at after your day on the river, Mineral Springs Pizza Pub & Grill. Old owner Ray sat by the front window each day drinking Pabst Blue Ribbon longnecks. Because of Ray's beer preference, PBR longnecks have long been a staple at the bar. Although I've never met Ray, I know that I like him.

The Mineral Springs Pizza Pub & Grill is known to locals as "the Springs". As you enter, you are greeted by aerial photos of both Spartan Stadium and the Big House (so "Go Green! Go White! Go Canoeing!" and "Let's Go Blue! Let's Go Paddling!"). The tavern gets its name from the springs at the well underneath the bar sign, next to the parking lot and on the south side of the pub.

Originally called Milt's Liquor Bar, the pub's early owners offered lodging right next door in "our new steam-heated cabins" after a night of dancing in Milt's "gold room on a smooth floor". This bar is resilient: built in the 40s, burnt down 40 years later, and then immediately rebuilt. Only recently were the last of Milt's lodges torn down.

Under the sign is the source of the springs at Mineral Springs Pub

The free popcorn will tide you over until the burgers and pizza arrives. The burgers are always fresh, never frozen, and Maggie sez they're the best she's had in a long time (a sentiment echoed in online reviews). We agreed that the Springs pizza was excellent right out of the oven – and the leftovers were still great hours later. After grabbing a bite, you can shoot some pool, play darts, or get in a game or two of table-top shuffleboard.

Owner Paul (Paulie) Kurtzman and his staff of Jody and Phil are welcoming folks. Between the warm treatment and the good chow & drink, you'll want to come back whether there's a Pine River trip involved or not. Mineral Springs Pizza Pub and Grill is located at 21257 Mackinaw Trail (aka as Old US Hwy 31) in Tustin MI 49688, 8 miles south of Cadillac. Phone (231) 829-4040, www.mineralspringspizzaandgrill.com. From downtown Tustin, take 20 Mile Road east to the stop sign, turn north (left) and travel 1 & 1/2 miles. The tavern will be on your left.

Horina Canoe & Kayak Rental

Horina Canoe & Kayak Rental is located on M37, 2 miles south of M55, a few feet south of the Pine River, 10 minutes east of downtown Wellston and 21 miles west of Cadillac. Horina's has been helping paddlers enjoy a day or two on the Pine River since 1965. Jim Horina is the livery owner, taking over from his parents in 1980.

Whether you like to paddle through the challenging rapids near Peterson Bridge in the Lower Pine, through the (relatively) calmer waters by Edgetts Bridge in the Upper Pine, or maybe somewhere between the two, Horina Canoe & Kayak Rental can match your paddling ability with the appropriate stretch of the river, making sure that your Pine journey is both fun and safe.

Of the 6 fine liveries that service the river, Horina is the one that helped make the Pine experience of our crack research team a successful one. A complete list of all Pine River liveries may be found on the next page.

Horina Canoe & Kayak Rental has 86 Old Town (Royalex) canoes and 30 kayaks, all 17' craft that they can rent to you. You won't find a tube to rent at Horina's because for most folks, the Pine is too cold for that mode of transportation ("I chilled my hiney on the piney"). Although the popularity of kayaks has exploded in the early-2000s, demand for canoes at Horina's still leads the way: Jim's rentals run 80% canoes and 20% kayaks.

Horina uncomplicates your trip by placing your vehicle downstream at any place you'd like them to OR let them meet you at the end point of your river trip, where you'll leave your car, truck or van, then catch a ride with Horina to your upstream launch site... and then paddle until you see your vehicle.

Jim Horina's favorite section of the Pine to paddle is the 3 hour run from Peterson Bridge to Low Bridge. For experienced paddlers (too many rapids and rocks for beginners), our crack research team agrees 100% with Jim.

The funniest customer request that Jim has had over the years was from a lady who called to make a reservation. She and her husband were coming in for a 3-day trip on the Pine, and they needed to know where the nearest Kentucky Fried Chicken was. The couple did get in their 3-day river trip, but Jim never did find out if they made the 20 mile one way trip to Cadillac for their KFC fix.

Horina Canoe & Kayak Rental is at 9889 M37 in Wellston, Michigan 49689. Jim Horina can be contacted at (231) 862-3470 or you email him at horinacanoes@yahoo.com. Take a look at Horina's website, which includes an excellent map of the Pine River journey, at www.horinacanoe.com.

PINE RIVER CANOE & KAYAK LIVERIES

From east to west...

Walker Bridge Canoe Livery (part of Paddlesports) (231) 862-3471
www.thepineriver.com/pine-river/walker-bridge-canoe-livery
Shomler Canoes & Kayaks (231) 862-3475 www.shomlercanoes.com
Horina Canoe & Kayak Rental (231) 862-3470 www.horinacanoe.com
Pine River Paddlesports Center (231) 862-3471 www.thepineriver.com
Bosman's Pine River Canoe Rental (231) 862-3661 www.bosmancanoe.com
Enchanted Acres Canoe & Campground (231) 266-5102 www.enchantedacrescamp.com

PINE RIVER CAMPGROUNDS & OTHER LODGING

Camping on the riverbanks (east to west)...

Silver Creek (231) 745-4651 (state)
Lincoln Bridge (231) 745-4651 (state)
Coolwater (231) 862-3481 www.coolwatercampground.com (private)
Peterson (231) 723-2211 (federal)
Pine River Paddlesports Center (231) 862-3471 www.thepineriver.com (private)
Loomis Landing Campground & Marina (231) 848-7449 www.loomislanding.com (private)
US Forest Service Camp Site 41 (231) 723-2211 (federal)

Cabins & Camping off-river (east to west)...

Coyote Crossing Resort (231) 862-3212 www.coyotecrossingresort.com
Kestelwoods Campground (231) 862-3476 www.kestelwoodscampground.com
Sportsman's Port (231) 862-3571 www.sportsmansport.com
Peterson Creek Cabins & Camping (231) 862-3508 www.petersoncreek-cabins.com
Twin Oaks Campground & Cabins (877) 442-3102 www.twinoakscamping.com
Buehler's Buck Stop (231) 848-4307

Rental cabins on the riverbanks (east to west)...

Logjam (231) 829-3727 www.logjamonthepine.com
Edgetts Lodge (248) 894-5115 www.edgettslodge.com

PINE RIVER: DIRECTIONS TO PUBLIC ACCESS POINTS

From east to west...

1. **Edgetts**: from US131 exit 168 (Tustin) drive west on 20 Mile Road for 5&1/2 miles to Raymond Road and turn left (south). It is 3 miles to the Pine River. 1/10th of a mile before (north of) the Pine, turn right (west) on to the dirt road just north of the tin house. On the dirt road take the left fork to the river. Poison Ivy lines the walking path to the Pine, so stay on the path. The last 50' to the river takes you down a steep walkway – so steep that it is suggested that you scout this out prior to descending while carrying canoes, kayaks, and other gear. An option to launching at Edgetts is to launch at the user-friendly Briar Patch access, 30 minutes downstream from Edgetts.

2. **Briar Patch**: from US131 exit 168 (Tustin), drive west on 20 Mile Rd. for 5&1/2 miles to Bristol (Raymond Road). In Bristol, 20 Mile Road becomes 8 Mile Road. Continue west on 8 Mile Road for 2 miles, going past the Sadler Road intersection, to the big bend left (south) as 8 Mile Road becomes Skookum Road. Follow Skookum Road south for 2 miles to, shortly after crossing the Pine, 5 Mile Road. Turn left (east) on to 5 Mile Road, taking it for 2 miles until it dead ends at the river.

3. **Meadowbrook**: from US131 exit 168 (Tustin), drive west on 20 Mile Road for 5&1/2 miles to Raymond Road and turn left (south). Take Raymond Road for two miles to 6 Mile Road and turn right (west). Drive 2 miles to the Pine River. The dirt path access is on your left, just before the Pine, at the SE corner of where the river flows below 6 Mile Road.

4. **Skookum North**: following the directions to Briar Patch, take Skookum Road south to the first right (west) turn north of the Pine River and follow the road to the access.

5. **Skookum South**: following the directions to Briar Patch, take Skookum Road south to 6 Mile Road. Turn right (west) on to 6 Mile and drive for 1/4 mile to the first right (north) turn, Pine River Road. Follow this road to the access.

6. **Walker**: from US131 exit 168 (Tustin), drive west on 20 Mile Road for 8 miles, 2 miles past Bristol, to Sadler Road and turn right (north). Take Sadler for one mile to 9 Mile Road and turn left (west). Follow 9 Mile Road until it ends at State Road. Turn left (south) on to State Road and in one minute the access at the Walker Bridge Canoe Livery will be on your right.

7. **Lincoln**: following the directions to Walker, take 9 Mile Road west until it ends at State Road. Turn right (north) at State Road and drive for 1 mile. The access road will be on your left, directly across State Road from the sign for 10 Mile Road.

8. **Elm Flats**: following the directions to Walker, take 9 Mile Road west until it ends at State Road. Turn right (north) at State Road and drive 4 miles to County Road 5230 and the sign to Elm Flats - turn left to the access. Coming from the north and the M55/M37 junction, take M37 South 2.5 miles to 48&1/2 Street (Kestelwoods Restaurant corner) and turn left (east). Follow 48&1/2 Street for 4 miles, crossing the Pine at the Dobson access, as it becomes W 50 Road. Take W 50 to the stop sign at 11&1/4 Road and turn right (south). Elm Flats is in 2 miles on your right.

9. **Dobson**: from the M55/M37 junction, take M37 South 2.5 miles to 48&1/2 Street (Kestelwoods Restaurant corner) and turn left (east). Follow 48&1/2 Street for 2 miles, crossing over the Pine on Dobson Bridge and turn left (south) into the access parking lot.

10. **Peterson**: from the M55/M37 junction, take M37 South for 1.5 miles. Just before crossing the Pine River, turn left (east) and drive to the access. The U.S. Forest Service Campground is across the river on the south bank.

11. **Low**: from the M55/M37 junction, take M55 west for 4.5 miles to the Roadside Park on the left (south) just before crossing over the Pine. Drive into the park and the access is in 1/2 mile.

12. **Norman-Dixon** (Tippy Dam): from the M55/M37 junction, take M55 west for 6 miles to Snyder Road and turn right (north). Take Snyder for 1.5 miles to Robinson Road (at the "Tippy Pond Boat Ramp" sign) and turn right (east). Follow Robinson Road for 1/2 mile to the access.

Paddling & Camping Checklist

"Plan thoroughly, but be prepared to follow the current"

for a day trip...

first aid kit

river shoes & dry shoes

bug spray

2 sets of vehicle keys

$$$ & wallet

dry clothes

dry (waterproof) bags

food

water

rain poncho

plastic drop cloths (for rain)

trash bags

knife

bungee cords

camera

sunglasses

sun block

cooler & ice

towels

clothesline rope

zip locks (large & small)

baseball cap

toilet paper

add for overnights...

tent

sleeping bag

blankets & pillows

thermarest/air mattress

mattress pump

campsite chairs

flashlights

forks/spoons/plates

can opener

grill & grate

pots/pans/large spoon

fire starters & matches/lighters

hand towels

Reynolds wrap (for leftovers)

soap, toothpaste/toothbrush

dish soap/scrub brush

Frisbees

euchre decks

nose strips (for snoring friends)

ear plugs (for snoring friends)

About the Author: Doc Fletcher

"Paddling Michigan's Pine: Tales from the River", is Doc's 6th book about canoeing and kayaking through Michigan and Wisconsin. Along with his wife Maggie (pictured here together along the banks of the Huron River), Doc travels across Michigan sharing river adventures at libraries and nature centers.

Doc's first 5 books, all published by Arbutus Press, are "Weekend Canoeing in Michigan", "Michigan Rivers Less Paddled", "Canoeing and Kayaking Wisconsin", "Paddling Michigan's Hidden Beauty", and "Michigan's Pere Marquette River: Paddling Through Its History"

For a source about all things canoeing and kayaking in Michigan, check out Maggie and Doc's website, www.canoeingmichiganrivers.com

Printed in the United States
By Bookmasters